Brody Parish Craig's *The Patient is an Unreliable Historian* begins on script, the patient diagnoses the failures of medicine. From the clinic to the prison cell, this book speaks through those abandoned or abused by systems of care. Craig's words alight with a madness that has both the fervid imagination of a raveling mind and a lucid anger forged in struggle. With a poet's lyricism and a critic's cutting insight, Craig carves queer possibilities into the open road between Oklahoma, Texas, and Arkansas. Here, freedom is a covenant we make with one another—a promise "to keep / us each alive." —V. Jo Hsu, author of *Constellating Home: Trans and Queer Asian American Rhetorics*

*The Patient is an Unreliable Historian* subverts everything we think about madness and what it means to be a patient. A beautiful, haunting, and tender lyrical memoir by Brody Parrish Craig. —Alice Wong, author of *Year of the Tiger*

A scheduled ghost—an ecstatic poet for this strange era, Brody Parrish Craig's *The Patient is an Unreliable Historian* is a collection of devotions. The poet writes, "I am limited / to the memorial / of language," and these poems go ahead and build their own shrines anyway. Another poet of the ecstatic, Allen Ginsberg wrote, "I saw the best minds of my generation destroyed by madness, starving hysterical naked." Now, it's Craig who catalogues the destruction by state-sanctioned violence. In each poem, a prayer—not to any gods but us. Not to any gods but transsexuals, addicts, the disabled, queers, beloveds, lilacs, and tenderness. This book is not a memorial, it is a march. —Canese Jarboe, author of *SISSY*

Brody Parrish Craig's *The Patient is an Unreliable Historian* contains a lyric both dazzling in its calm and tender in its storm. The speaker in Craig's poems knows the body as an intimate archive of potential: "& maybe I'm going / under the knife / to sing with other angels." This is an exercise in autonomy, in liberation for the love of personhood. The joy in this collection is free from economy and lives in the commons: "say pennies lie / peonies grow." —C.T. Salazar, author of *Headless John the Baptist Hitchhiking*


Like the poet Frank Stanford, Brody Parrish Craig is a singular, urgent voice born of the South. But Craig grew up in a different battlefield, an unbuckled Bible Belt, where Americans "made the missing into headlines" and "played the prison like a savior." This is an America where the body becomes a "criminal," the hospital isn't a "safe space," "cis- subtitle / our language," and barriers "keep disabled / out." Craig's poetry has a distinct vision that trespasses borders and punctuations, breathes revolution and evolution. *The Patient Is an Unreliable Historian* is a collection of psalms, "the split husk sacrament" where if you "hold / the notes so long / the sound unblocks / each door you know // your future possible / as a newly unbarred window." Craig writes, "I'll punch the door they shut us in / until the copper melts." These poems are our guidebook to that other America. —Kaveh Bassiri, author of *99 Names of Exile* and *Elementary English*

PREVIOUS BOOK

*BOYISH* (Omnidawn, 2021)

# THE PATIENT IS AN
# UNRELIABLE HISTORIAN

Cover design by Maximiliano Calabotta & Joshua R. Johnson
Cover typeface: Garamond
Interior design by Laura Joakimson
Interior typeface: Warnock Pro and Adobe Garamond

Library of Congress Cataloging-in-Publication Data

Names: Craig, Brody Parrish, 1991- author.
Title: The Patient is an Unreliable Historian / Brody Parrish Craig.
Description: Oakland, California : Omnidawn Publishing, 2024. | Summary:
"The poems of Brody Parrish Craig's new collection upends narratives
around current psychiatric treatment models to focus on the lived
experience of survivors and to speak toward liberation, abolition, and
disability justice. Titled after the author's own medical records, The
Patient Is an Unreliable Historian questions the prevailing narrative
that the medical industry knows stories of disability and madness better
than those who have lived them. Craig uses lyricism to expose the
intersection of madness and criminality in contemporary American
culture, moving through institutions, community spaces, and loss of kin.
Through the course of the collection, the speaker turns toward
irreverence and interrogation, carves out their own freedom, and
challenges the script of the patient, the mad, and the "criminal." These
poems deconstruct the "patient" to set the person free"-- Provided by
publisher.
Identifiers: LCCN 2024012866 | ISBN 9781632431530 (trade paperback)
Subjects: LCSH: Patients--Poetry. | Medicine--Practice--Poetry. | LCGFT:
    Poetry.
Classification: LCC PS3603.R348 P38 2024 | DDC 811/.6--dc23/eng/20240322
LC record available at https://lccn.loc.gov/2024012866

Published by Omnidawn Publishing, Oakland, California
www.omnidawn.com
10 9 8 7 6 5 4 3 2 1
ISBN: 978-1-63243-153-0

# THE PATIENT IS AN UNRELIABLE HISTORIAN

Brody Parrish Craig

OMNIDAWN PUBLISHING
OAKLAND, CALIFORNIA
2024

# Contents

**Mad in America**
*after Robert Whitaker*

Bellevue of the Ball, I court myself & off the record
we are made of mustard powder, seeds, and *blister*
*in the madhouse son*—eighth notes of a Quaker's tale
& promise they can't keep. To rewrite health as lock-up,
1800's number you can call. 1-800- symptomatic sun.

A fresh script caged between, a bloodline's malady/I'm leeching off
the social ladder. Centuries, the 21st appointment with the warden.
Who's unhinged meaning who needs to be locked in the hospital--
who's crazy, talking now, their manneristic mouth a danger

to themselves: we could be blue. We could be made of cloth
all swaddled up and open in the back, the rows of visions,
could be prophets, sick things, could be taken down the hall

to let shock's light in—Enlightenment to let the leeches out—
the water spinning with a cure contraption—Take us by the collar
to the mouth. A gag's restraint. So patient in our sickness

& in health, we could be ward-robe in the stars,
*The Snake Pit* screening other's racing thoughts.
Who came and went, all body & all mind, all asymmetrical,
all necklines built for shock, even the white dressed socialite.

Her husband bought a matching clutch of white sheet for the gown.
Mistaken as Bellevue or Bethlehem, who sprouted blisters there.

We cling to white walls looking for a scripture, vine-clawed eyes,
a creeper in the window looking back in night mare's stable house.

A modest fee to watch the patients rise. A ticket
for the fair grounds keep. To see the bloodline
never worthy of a free ride—build up of zoos—

this cripple carnival—this caged & patient sunrise—
& this symptomatic sun—the patience oversaturated, full,
the mad house without blankets, cast of clouds, who will I keep—

this 1800th line:    *Call if you experience this moon as for the madman—*

**In The Last Episode**

*I stole hir car & wound up barefoot in the sticks—*
                    *there was no river but my tongue—*


A few weeks before Easter, I was on the highway
cruising toward a month endeavor that would mark
my last stint in the wards. When I took off in my girlfriend's car,
the destination was evasion. After years of more than panic
drugs abuse self-loathing fear, now the trauma turned
to paranoia like an engine. On the brink of break, I took
her keys from our apartment's kitchen counter. Mid-episode,
I ran that white horse engine ragged for a good three days.

From a liquor store's neon cowboy marquee off 62 & up,
I drove westward to Oklahoma's border, lost cell phone service,
signal, somehow landed on a dirt road. Dead stopped in the center
overgrown, another empty street. I took down an abandoned building's
address, clapboard, shotgun. Jotted on the blank space
of some ripped-out poem's title page. Looking back, indicative,
to mark some future in the margins. Regardless, there is always hope of home.

\*\*\*
\*\*\*
\*\*\*


I woke up in another Exxon lot going nowhere, whereabouts unknown.
I dropped my laptop out the window due to surveillance on the frontroad,
hopped onto the highway, headed toward Texas, just to see JC,
made cheap talk on our cells, some breakfast stop, one stateline then the other,
furthered on by first-light. Suddenly, I turned around.

\*\*\*
\*\*\*

***

*Dodge emptied of fuel—my mouth & I were on the run—*

Who knows what hit. When sun came,
or soon after, in Missouri,
gas'd run out. I'd ditched the car,
took off on foot, & mid-day hitched
a ride with some dykedriver in the semi.

Something about my language
seemed to freak dykedriver out.
I was talking about the pipeline,
about the camps, other allusions

often best left to assumption,
not discussion, among strangers,
I had assumed the reasonable position
shh/e could read into it all
until the moment when shh/e dropped
me off—& I kept moving.

Nobody knows when I hit the motel,
but soon after, I'd spent my last buck
on a fast meal, realizing my ID, my money,
all was lost—or perhaps absent—the entire time.

***
***
***

By nightfall, up & running, I was spotted
in a Walmart lot nearby. The cops came
according to the shopping center's desires
to pick somebody up outside itself
for peace-disturbing, I hustled toward the street
until I ripped my shirt off to evade arrest.

They can't touch me, everybody thinks, until, *they could.*

\*\*\*
\*\*\*
\*\*\*

*But if there'd been a river*

> *I would've crossed over—*
> *I would've named it renaissance,*

*Euphrates, genesis—*

From sleepless nights in county jail,
they transport us by ambulance

a state-ward calling everybody home
once, after all, invisible,

indivisible by walls all
creatures kept inside their cells—
outside their cells, themselves,
they are no better off

*unhinged.*
*unhinged.*


*unhinged.* After a stint,
some will resurface,
stripped again—
searching for the moment
when the world ran out
or runs out, returning here
again to beg permission
into inhibited space—
selective institutions—
schools, the workforce,

housing, jobs: always give them notice
when you will lose them funds
or time, always given notice
you will lose your funds
or time, and time again,
and energy, discrimination
only definition
& everybody knows
that all we've gained
a questionable understanding
as to whether you are eligible
to enter here or anywhere
by all affairs is up to warning,
power, others—uncertainty is to exist
amongst those keeping tabs here,
here in every file & chart,
the single file your body held:
the single file your walk,
the single file your line,
the single file your chart,
the single file your line-up,
the single file your feet,
your hands, your memory.
It's in your hands.
the single file it seems
nobody held

\*\*\*
\*\*\*
\*\*\*


*Instead the passage was a shoulder—gravel in-between—*

Because the meds were off,
because we've all done this before,
Because I went to the local ER
to get adjusted in dire straits & time.

Because the doctor misunderstood the script
Because he prescribed a double-lethal dose
Because, technically, he refilled your medication

Because technically, you caught it first,
and only then you somehow stayed alive,
Because technically, it was too late,
Because the ambulance tailed you from the start

Because it's only luck & your own good
For your own good

Because it's carnal knowledge
to catch the error as they went to fill

Because I couldn't fix the script
It's god's predestination—time—

Back on the run & screaming 4/4/4 on the college sponsored byway
Back on the run & channeling some sort of consciousness I couldn't speak

I couldn't unspeak anything
or anymore. On Easter Sunday,
I left a local bank by police escort,
then, now & again, with X number of days,
I will re-enter

doubled ward.

\*\*\*
\*\*\*
\*\*\*

*My clouded blue, eyes manic—signs of periodic visioning—*

Five years into the future, I'm writing this to keep
us each alive. I'm writing this to tell you what we're made of.

\*\*\*
\*\*\*
\*\*\*

*In some condition   when I crossed back*

   *into the traffic—*

      *rusted nails & god so near my feet—*

We woke up to the near future, & trichotillomanic dreams.
We woke up in 3 am dark heat feeling hair pulled
from between our teeth, the clog of rat's nest pushed
from throat in dream.

X on the dresser, on the carpet,
on the ceiling vents, we woke.

A parking lot of visitors in mind.

We woke up with 3 bodies: yours, a strange old woman's mask, and mine.
We woke up with a papier-mâché forehead

& a fearful, five-year miracle:    *Stigmatized & grandiose,*

   *I could've been a portrait—*

            *I could have*

*been a painting—*

*not to touch—*

Before sound or light begins,
today releases you, & just as timed.
Breaks cycles dawns holds on.

Before me, a hippocampus, a haywire, a barn swallow,
circle, pattern on the ceiling fan. Nights can't distinguish what
(or how) we've done, so far, along. Breaking laps of river's street-edge.
Laugh of current's call. Circadian. Rhythm. Playgue. Cicada
huddlebed. When I wake & wave

to write you down into me,
not revising every memory.
The room is dimly lit—bulb set
like clock beside the altar.

My partner wakes & calls me back
to bed, to blank sheets, blue & bright

I unfold from. The supermoon is seamless—
cloud-night covers efface all, no lines, no point
of view to pin down, termed horizon. Time unsealed.

Zones away, another wakes.
Some routine noise as no alarm here.

*It's an adjustment, understated, to recreate light years, linears with time.*

Routine coffee? 4am. Routine day? At nightfall.
This morning, I am driving with them back
to Oklahoma—another dream. We drive
for accidental hours. No one decides this way.

In my handed-down Honda, we cross the border
into Westville, 5 years to the teeth. The clock reads
April 2nd. *My soul crosses here five years old.* An anniversary

gift: gas station near the church I parked my car, the town
center where I watched the party-goers dance inside, then drove
to Houston, Austin, Cassville, in between. & *Here, I am, alive*

& with it—a different seat inside the heart
to see the landscape & keep going, see what
must be precise*, accidental*, same,
say, backroad, outside the window, know
this moment as *returning, back*.

Traveling backwards, *wards*,
not as still there, but still

not,

*there*. A flash back under reams
until the lights click off. The dream
lands different. Here. *A healing spell*
*cast into eyelids. a dozen plus sheets*,

to the coming wind—

## Handle (Jowl Is Clean)

the aftermath so high
noon spurns the door
into the rubble—handle

jowl is clean come off
the cringe as pill roll
smooth to pebble off

the tongue a script
I stole to skim the haze
another framesworn off

conclusion: blackbirds flew against the windows

strikethrough & struckthrough
the quiet down on glass
to keep us soundproof

the stones throw away

house & driest hide
I found us open crevice
need

no key to place
the underside
the stairwelltooth
the secret
mouth hinge

whereabouts
unknown
I carve
box cold

this unkeptskeleton

I keep
beneath
no cabinets
medicine

some locket flesh
& ribbed groan

early jolt
awake from curing dream

## Thorazine at 10:00 am

Nobody told the river *run from what you're made of.*
The bramble on & on for miles. On the rocks, unsteady
hem of riverbank. I know by now exquisite gowns
wide open in the back. Old fashioned hospital. The bills

all churning yellow as a heron's mouth. I'm out to lunch,
some charted water along the bridge of doctor's nose.
His finger pushes spectacles. He's troubled by my wonder.
All the daisies I have chained around my neck. He pulls them up

right as he concentrates. I keep my hands behind my back.
I get what's given. Single file. Some charted water like a miracle
they could have fed the thousands—pristine scripts and pills.
A guardrail on my shoulder, miles & miles. Before I fall

asleep, I dream they gravel every blue thread in the dark.
The bus comes like a flower in the rain.

**The Quiet Room**

I never came to. And I never came to know
the deer jowl like a padlock. Whoever hid the key
along the brink of someone's mouth to make a quiet room.
Whoever said this god as stray's revival. Quick return

of warded invoice in the mail, a doctor's voicemail
trailing dark, too toward with you, the flash flood rush
unreined. The clobbered mountain top. Unbelted bible,
funny sediment of prayer & enemy rich soil: Some speaker

blaring in the silver in the sliver of the holler.
*I steeped the savior in a barrel, I crossed my eyes along the strain.*
Even-keeled again, a seedy smirk through orchard, eden-
tongued. A song, you break it open. Crumbled veins, you break

a sweat. Horizonless as it is dark,
you hydroplane into another's house.
You do not enter as you.
Do not enter. Simile for gate—

cinched-off, somewhat accountable.
What comes back around: A tickhound
waiting on your doorstep. Nurses. Clockwork.
River: river. *Run.* A witness feed itself

& gathering up every buckeye
you will hold up luck & holler

out to lunch again, strike through negated
bramble crown king's river with a thorn—
ungodly given thing, this straight-laced
jacket's nest. The needless sting
& mad-dash fence amongst these needles.
I hear they called the hospital. Now, run

from what you're made of: thrush adrenaline
in thorn, the undergutted     chicken coop,
that wire house, the fence hinged rib.
the heartland.

**Funny Farm**

Some gods as more than rhythm
in the purple streak of trees—unbruised—
what works for you, it may not work for me,
this doppelganger god.

Inside I was a key that someone swallowed once.

**Chromosomes to Name the Wild**

X marks the spot the carve initials here
my start of letters red clay mud rouge scratch
into the trees your pocket knife whittles
indention away parts you can't pronounce

the scar ruts in my landscape broken down
to blood cell don't abbreviate the river
don't call the ruddy body *close enough*
if stream's excess fills shines close

to copper & to touch red clay dirt water
once my mother mentioned wilderness
grandfather taught me how to tell
the difference: what one must & must'nt keep

keep determining & don't you try to name the wild
bank on the silt beside us scabbing back

## JC the Exxon Baptist Can Walk on Water If

given clear directions he crosses the surface
full of split white lines passes the blue
bastards' first test then takes another lick
from blotter's height of blur across the water
find him out near heaven & then back beside the ducks
Deleuze, kratom, full pack inside the pond
mouthing off at angels pearly gates one bastard's cuffs
then lined with silver on the water-bank near dawn
the fishermen saw it all—before he told us resurrect—
before he totaled father's pick-up in the pond

crossing intersections named after Kings & man we knew
it was a symbol that'd tipped him off into the passage
pond's shallow offer through the water he saw it all down there
the fish a dozen men like us another god school jumper

swinging kicking clay reciting sunday childhood's apparition
all our gospel flapping in the wind

## The News

they tell us nobody jumped
nobody flinched a goddamn minute

they tell us the good news
& then nobody asks

what surfaces as evidence
& breaking flash

someone will claim us soon
& they will make us into parable

to call it faith: to cross
both feet as we fly over flood

## Holy Rollers
*after Frank Stanford*

the night I drank so much
burgundy I popped
a tire on the mailbox
the pastel pink clapboard
house smelled of pancakes
cat piss your cologne
we broke into the cemetery
to see how the dead were doing
we dropped Ezekiel bread to homeless
men downtown leaving the alley
with our sack you listed off the Saints'
stats spent your change on biblical
allusions on ingredients you cooked
another testament another loaf
& spoke on miracles that Jesus put
you through or put through to you
we fed the 1000s weed & wheat
as you stockpiled your father's guns
in the bread box for the FEMA camp
round up to come that summer
when I wrapped my joints in bible paper
if the rollers ran out in our makeshift motel
I talked a good game about angels flapping
my mouth like a wing my sedan circling
the bus depot looking for a man
to give a good meal we'd sell the sack
then buy a bag of sprouted grain
& barley wine to make the night stop spilling
over Highland you proselytized
inside the shuttered speedtrap
of apocalypse & god these nights
I wonder if you knew—know—what's to come of us—again
your temple bulging like a coffin-bell—face ringing come to supper—
holding everybody up through Shreveport dawn

**Cross-Examination**

who sopped up the river
who broke up the bread
who slit the cat's eye
who ate the orchard
who bought a lemon
& who drove it fast
who climbed a tree
who caught a case of leaves
that looked just like
your father's father
who caught a fish
& complimented god
who broke the mold
when he made that one
who everybody called son
or else called son of a gun

**Before the Prodigal Returns**

Used to get my kicks from slicing lemons, forearms, tangerines.
All pain & pleasure in the eye of the beholder.

Last month was a bad spell. Dawn felt like a blood pact.
I cut up with wrong gods; spilled my temper up a creek:
a pool of motor oil. Crude puddle that could never leave the bed.

My temples stayed so tense I couldn't see the light of day without
an aspirin on the hour. Sensitivity to sun & other phenom of the spring,
my dry throat & my wet iris, my throat sore as a thumb not green,
some savior in my head kept flipping tables, saying *please, now, listen,
stop—this mine—you're mine—my sanctuary*—of a child who keeps
on sobbing over the spilled milkweed: the truth lives inside my neck

of woods, there's never been a lost cause garden—
before the prodigal returned, his tatted arms were open

*pain for glory* vining up his biceps when he walked
across our neighborhood to plant himself at midnight

on our doorstep freshly cut & without water. hand-delivered rose,
his throat slit as a red horizon slit as the door I cracked a slight
slit as my eyes, what neither could announce: it was his eyes
only his eyes that asked to be let in. pill-bugged, dilated,
weed-whacked, us the color of hot coals I pressed
against his neck a butterfly a bandage as his body
shadowboxed along the flutter of my hands.

I pressed against as baby stuttered *shit—man shit—
stand still—*or—*don't you call the doctor trippin'*
until sunrise & morning came up after all. I broke the earth
into a shallow bed of pepper plants, the stoop of prayer & feel of soil
as prayer for weeds to leave again without another warning.
Someday, the prodigal came back with a fresh shave

& *faith* tattooed in block across the neckline's cut.
A promised seal over the same old shovel's scar.

Despite, we pulled & pulled—another blossom without name.
We listened for the dirt turn like a cheek all summer long
but couldn't see the miracle: to see this same truth within planted seed
as unseen weed which harbors sprout—a berry or the blossom made
so obvious, so obstinate, that no one'd cared to know
their given names.

**"I'll Go In The Morning"**

I'm clicking your obituary closed
as harmless search
as browser window's hotbox funeral
as overdose rolled up in google
as another deadly tubed machine.

Your body's two months deep.
Can't know who never came but me.
To take you in as browser's splurge.
We'll never cover you. One body went.
Another stayed—gray shirt of his inside my closet.

I put on the material & keep it on—
then, hover the donation box. Can I? Abrupt
& punked, God's drag queen dress again.
Another diva lost to funeral. Never an official
address to rhinestone patch the gauze.

To drop Naloxone, test strips, who will call
your first name now. After the cause & death,
your sister whirs her own thin sheet of static
electricity across the city, each of us nameless
as lightning bugs circling the in-patient yard.

Or so I read to numb. Or so I read your name on google.
Or so when they call the election "harm-reduction"
I'll hear the click of calls he forwarded after
I'd finally just found him a bed. This side of heaven,
they'll co-opt our front stoop where the quiet lives,

the peace before a boy returns to thunder,
stomping grounds, a whim for wind to ride & clutch
of dial tone, rehab's number still inside one hand
the casket couldn't close. His voice & smell

material, then immaterial. Gone or passed along.

I tell god that he won't go until the morning.

**Tracy**

Your chair is empty in the middle of the room.
The fabric of everything is blue.

When your face blues into sun, Heaven is not everything.
Heaven is you huffing

breath within the Georgia noon. Heaven is the orb weaver
making strides along my window. Silk-thread of stimulant

along the eyelid in the dark, is god more than a welfare check?
Another door without an answer. Your body's burning question.

Flaming as queer Alabam. Last night, we made a deal
across the fog. & You are here. Your hands nailed in my hands.

A hand layed on the threshold. Your hands tattooed my forearm.
Your hands layed on my windowsill. Fireside, that night, you left the chair.

And then, we said: I see your body's runoff moonlight.
And then, we said: Listen—I'll be right back.

And then, we burned your obit in the fire.
And then, I did not see the chair. Tracy, I saw your hands.

## Babylon

*Some nights the light relapses.*
A bitter dogwood & the barking door.

when Jesus comes too soon
to croon his neck out at the audience,

he false-starts. Turns around.
Puts all behind him. Simply put,

Jesus decides against the resurrection.
Unknowingly, he leaves

a pillow book entombed.
The rest is Word some king rewrote

to leave us with the word of god.
Fact checked for centuries,

we're still here waiting on return.
Give it a rest, expensive fable.

Give it a rest. To rest, somebody leaves
their sentence struck-through on the dash.

Posthumous text when my acrylics click
the keyboard, free EMDR in morning light.

I babble on
to end the story of its running mouth.
The brook waves back.

Some running header, the horizon sought
its document. I guess

that I'm still here
still placing words into your tired mouth.

Here hanging out in Babylon
with your long-bottled lip

of synonyms, the paper trails
that shuffle by my door,

A scheduled ghost.
A textless thread of close

*Calls clinging to your teeth like dogwood blossoms.*

**What Held**

in plain sight dagger held in the light of day that cuts
through heavens intersection

at the crossroads
one brave woman
almost meets his knife

his white hand held
as if his blood was on the line
because her eyes met his
my body caught beside her
as I run from the sidewalk
to the traffic light

suburban common
nothing notable
unless

& then until the car stops

shadow of a man
we can't outrun

sudden
& sharp
he jerks
the driver door

the centuries that came
within the gnash of blade
his teeth shit grin
of generations
eyes hot flame across
the intersection burning

cross into the blade he held
as close as notion he could turn
a black woman to a ghost
with no recourse

the cops show up
to keep him free
from harm again
they question us
but never why
a knife could slice
through town

within a white man's hand
another white man

## Criminal

all eve, you double-fisted
pounding cell wall where
this passage ends—so what

on earth, was it, now, time?
the question of the decade
that we'd cussed everything

given—*I'm quitting drinking like*
*a cop, a plea in blues, some bitterness.*
uncertain where/if god came in

& took the wheel, so far, all gone,
you ever turned the tumbling earth
into a tumbler? ever bottled

necks in boxes, turned who's missing
water into wine? necessary, now,
we bruise. our knuckles still. our knuckles

bloodied, white as light some claim
they saw as they were coming "clean"—
my anger red as the last light I saw

before I sped the car back up.
*I'm quitting drinking like someone pulled*
*one over on me.* I'm punching doors
they shut until the copper melts.

\*\*\*
\*\*\*
\*\*\*

or don't. you won't.

hold still:
or else all eve, you'll have
these bloodied hands.

red burst of criminal
along the knuckles,

breaking out in bruise
of cell to cell

whose cell will state
or god defend

\*\*\*
\*\*\*
\*\*\*


in          so far,     all gone,

all time
to waste  wasted            I am
                                    I got
                                    I caught
                                    I served
                                    they gave
                                    & others
                                    sentence
                                    fool of euphemisms
symbolism's neck stuck back
into the local bars
then local bars

holding cells against the cell
the prison's body over yours & mine
& I got time to talk about
America of crated miracles

who turned well-spun wine for profit
who took up all the water
who made the missing into headlines
who played the prison like a savior
party trick rolled up a miracle

whose headlines rolled just like a joint
along the breakfast table

in the papers
we saw somebody
somewhere again got life

in the language
we will know
this means
the state just took
a life

we have seen these treatment programs
& we have seen who called them good
creation myth of cell which takes the cell
creation myth of life which takes a life

a single sentence
we have seen the definition of a body
shift into a prison

O America of fines
& fine print
of a "cell" over a cell
of a cell into a box into a cell
into a box into a cage into a box
into a cell

whose holding cells

whose holding us
who spent their $$$$$$$$$$$$$$$$
or their last dime

to buy a paper
full of false prophets
& cure-alls
media whose mass
of bars whose mass
who stirs the chalice full

the well-spun wine
who calls this body "criminal"

\*\*\*
\*\*\*
\*\*\*

who needs good news
when you really need a miracle

I'll punch the doors they shut us in
until the copper melts.

**Between No Man's Land & City Lights that Map Trip Wire. Stars.**

the deer. the deer that wrecked us. synecdoche for madmen
a settlement we coin a body "shy of sound" some animal
toss of phrase. to play, we sprout the marrow from the temple.
sound comes out. again the railroad tracks. we cross out or over
what will spring. a splinter from the mouth.
a sprint & us uncoming from the hooves.

the town's square body. gaping awe. what held the semi- up
across the bottleneck. the traffic & the cells flash
inch from antler—then, the flash of tail into the woods—
a headless image—my mind leaves by the skin of its teeth

unflung the water glass I broke you.  a door w/o a house.
            who comes unhinged like us.        to ward off branches.

when the buck stopped at the riverwalk,        they knew god as one
            inch from antler.        drawn out as your child's image

on the kitchen countertop.                who warrants a man:
a tick or mugshot held to window—
                        synapse slapped. the jailhouse doctor.
kept my mouth shut as an eye.        what held the key to every fifth

dimension. between no man's land & city lights that map trip wire. stars.

waiting never lasted.        we kept up. a nervous break
through fence.        the deer tipped off through wire.

to fill. in the blank mouth. no one attested.

                                what crouched in
        the crosswalk.
                                we showered in
        the ward's eye,

top to bottom in the last box.

       a finger tapped the water/cell tower's edge
impatient.

we are many generations.
searching for the riverneck. caught up in the border

                           where the bank rolled up w/ rain.

**"To Be in A Time of War"**
*after Etel Adnan*

to quit your day job, to go through the drive-thru, to tip the barista, to smile, to keep
smiling, to pick a friend up, to turn up the radio, to drive toward the lake, to briefly
lose signal, to reach the lake shore, to lose signal again, to sit by the lake shore, to touch
the lake shore, to hear the lake shore, to light the incense, to talk transition(s), to watch
the mosquito hawk, to watch the bird circle, to disperse the dandelion, to wish, to pray,
to breathe in deeply, to walk toward the car, to open the cell, to see your messenger, to
know another trans Arkansan dead, to send a crying emoji, to tell your friend, to check
on your partner, to send a crying emoji, to walk to the bathroom, to pause at the flower,
to send a crying emoji, to relight the incense, to walk in the stall, to send a crying emoji,
to do your usual business, to unlock the stall, to wash your hands, to return from the
bathroom, to put out the incense, to walk to the car, to write a full sentence, to replay the
moment, to send a crying emoji, to turn on the radio, to buckle your seat belt, to briefly
lose signal, to turn up the radio, to see the deer on your right, to briefly lose signal, to
briefly lose signal, to drive

### In Danger (To Myself & Others)

dagger, bullet, spark between our eyes we watch god's shape & holler point against clouds
the body made the news last night as television flickered static wrong inside each mouth
some evidence of grace summer of judges hearing sworn me another state commitment
without power bill of right winged birds & institutions piling up again & repetitious new
addition from the days of medic's tourniquet to noteworthy the piano sounds in seconds
tempo in the dayroom

treatment placed complexity unplanning this our triggers were two wound up bodies
fearing god & self this adult units stint acute as look I keep from glint of whiteboy's
sudden strike my body blocking the flailed dagger from youth's face then crotch heap that
the cops search stole from my delusions to the flesh a fresh assault

the sheetless twin now turned you kept your praise & worship & your love as antithetical
the common space around our dim the light switched plastic furniture & bruise my shin
kicked handprint & my eyes as beautiful your confidence & vocal tones

the likeness of my friends who held me two weeks in the clutch
their gentle fingers kissing god into my disappearance

\*\*\*
\*\*\*
\*\*\*

on the wing of warning sings now shoeless in borrowed cloth a week or less along the
road you flip the script & hear the lessons in my wrist
you teach me music months after they flipped the badge
& they said I was lot's wife in my loitering outside the hospital
trying to find a safe ride home no turning back
the blueboys came

& I will always be in cuffs & deep cut tracks the blue restraints
down to the bone—what I've unknown as point of view again

third person gone to lunch & war

\*\*\*
\*\*\*
\*\*\*

I can't sleep or be here now
the hallway's crevice tight beside myself my quiet mattress four walls taken to the floor
this fearful sketch will never be our common ground but every memory the new gods
some recall as nurses cameras monitor & half asleep another woman barges in the room
her body's overcast my own

some part time keeper said wake up listen don't you can't
sleep in the stark flesh here accidental as my body
what unblanketed & caught

into my unshared room
into my trans extracted double bed
into my flash to solitary & confinement
few days prior

\*\*\*
\*\*\*
\*\*\*

I won't let anyone bleed out
but on her watch its all wrong
pronouns in her mouth I can't
even shave my face w/o surveillance
I can't be trusted
with a tampon
my misunderstood
period then disclosure
but never closure

why do bodies need
occasional reprieve

each eye & fleshy hole so weary
can't save my ass
from the sockets spark again

this marginal
diss-association

you must feel
the scumbags
in our wake & wave

***
***
***

this misinterpreted revival
& the bible held adjacent to
your flood inside a little room
& one cot over an uncomforting

new patient who deepthroats
another damn banana between meals & twice now
for gratification never knowing the true root word for affection (much less mine)

what's graspless we can't fully know
what has ungrasped us now a hand that shakes
holding the lost ones felt
of worn down wash-tip marker

I am over 100 letters
I can't read

***
***
***

can't say or save

our names & you
can't fully see
me hurling pills
& hurling caution
signs across embodied huddle

I flail the yellowed plastic at the tech unfold my rage

behavioral to them


\*\*\*
\*\*\*
\*\*\*


this anger we wait to open our pockets with nothing left we never steal what turns to
shard the pointless spoon or cuddled styrofoam no knives or strings or rings just research
& a patient's song again on the piano my jointed yet disjointed lyric tucked inside your
pocket's lint

you gave me shoes that first day & I felt more than enough more than some man the
state turned out into a glasshouse with one soft tree along the distant yard your kindness
and the landscaper you kept inside your steady hands the mouth misread as eyes and bad
handwriting

words I said
some hedges
kept too crisp
you noted everything

in a black moleskine
you opened

let me read the pages
grinned

\*\*\*
\*\*\*
\*\*\*

the days we prayed barefoot along the cafeteria's woodgrain
the cherry stained & table free body that opened as the corner

when I close my eyes
three times each day
I croon to hum
I still remember you

how we stared after the throat held at the freeway
how we were so damned determined once again to feel alive

when mornings rose our fists up as the moon as what comes back what's leaving behind
those teargassed lids then tears & rage along the blueboys shoulders flashes and everyone
I know plus me's all acting up & spiraling down again

I'll know you deeply

just after a few days
when I'd circled salted soundtrack parking lot street-fulls

our overlap of holy words
when I paced the halls
as protests every hour

\*\*\*
\*\*\*
\*\*\*

every breath a revolution
these moments small
as weary back
in a clear cell
each morning

that we called the eye
and its attention
wasn't gone
but rootless
as another's
nuit blanche
commenced

\*\*\*
\*\*\*
\*\*\*

& nothing free

the way eves swell
I speak in crosswires

I am limited

I am limited
to the memorial
of language

\*\*\*
\*\*\*
\*\*\*

I'm lucky when I realize that the staff can't understand me if I speak French

I'm so lucky that I disappear

& you don't know me as the maple road
only as heady tongue vibration
pills as ominous communion rolled

beneath the wafered tongues

we play our sole possession
& the house goes crazy flipping dominoes


we never were the lepers but your mind
kept writing home


your notions sin—do you remember
when I fed you cilantro from my fork
that one calm in the cafeteria
the shuffle tender as you laughed


& we both laughed your bible off
as joy again
a moment
when my mind
stopped jumping itself
off the roof
again


\*\*\*
\*\*\*
\*\*\*


two months now the piano held
those powerlines I'll end
this trauma's war & I'll return
the institution's plastic


liminal now & then forget
just for a moment
what pissed me off


the metal toilet
& the bad photos
of trees we couldn't touch less keep
despite this prolonged glance

I heard you
& your body's
meditative bowl

\*\*\*
\*\*\*
\*\*\*


The small of hours after transport took me out
I asked what drained you too

stolen as we enter
this contact nebulous

I see you
now & again

keep in mind
our blown glass knees

what healed & prayed your body into silence
mine in stillness

without fear along god's grain

I hope you
hold what's close
take notes

on passages
deciphered,
untranslated:

the words another's voice pitched wrong
& you let go of

the queer inside you held like terror

held onto the bible by your bed


\*\*\*
\*\*\*
\*\*\*


I hope you return home
& recall worship music
praise we played those hymns

I hope you better yet possess
your own piano

I hope your future boyfriend drums
better than I could on the psych ward stools

that you keep the naked ear
from way back when
we tuned the furniture awake
or at least that when the music swims

you back to you again
that if all else you feel

what braided sound
from keys to hands

each open palm as psalm
& what moves past

beyond the throat

I hope you hold
the notes so long
the sound unblocks
each door you know

your future possible
as a newly unbarred window

## As If the Body Was

more than oyster, egg, a shell
we can't or won't crack up
you crack down on desire
a user manual for our vehicle

no need to be calibrated

our leaking fluid *grlboygrl*
outta whack & shaking on their highway

worried about the truck driver
flailing into my space my stance
my shoulder lane to say
*safe space safe space safe space*

& eve can't shut eye I can't stand
to hear that shut-I sound mudflap
thin skin over the soul
I'm up all night dark durable & spinning
another's slit-eye body like a marble
circling the text that says I am

no sculpture, object, seen
as singular, my neighbor's
feral cat & frozen as a still
from Buñuel's drama still
frame slice the lid just like a jar lid
review my notes again as foreign film
I'm here

& I'll tell you again
the cis- subtitle
our language

the gate kept nouns
who held my body's
future & violets cut

another tense bouqueted between my pearly whites

**I'll Star My Favorite Passages If We're Living in End Times**

is that a chemtrail or comet?
did millennials kill the pastoral?

if you're reading this you're live
streaming some creation myth

*I'm here to help you troubleshoot yr storm*
at the bookstore I witnessed

a white horse

men come
in red
laced boots

at exxon went librarian
of war scanning for shooters
anti-bodies in the margin
of my I

came here to recommend a brand
new dystopian novel
to execute escape

hatch tacked
into the fire
wall

what's to be trusted
when no one looks close

to alarm
in this town, no,
country, rather,

leaflets on
the second coming free
at every empty fuel
station

who booked you in
these cells

I lost
my mind
last night

night shifting
in a picket sign

asking now what
will mark the spot
that you will bank on

**Liminal Trespassing**

Lobotomize the lilacs.
Cut the body down to size.
Confine blue sky to solitary.
I spent a day across

the concrete:
a trespassed
criminal that's caught
outside denial
of urgent care.

They made me out for lock-up.
I made it out of concrete.
I made it off the sidewalk
by the skin of my own teeth.

\*\*\*
\*\*\*
\*\*\*

Somedays I clutch rosemary for salvation.
Tonight I wish to blow the blue lights out.

\*\*\*
\*\*\*
\*\*\*

Some flowers never mind.
Overgrown despite
fresh cut in the white vase.
Never mind
no weed will pull itself
from holy ground.

The operator
not the crisis
but the call.
A 911 discovery.

They pull our voice out from the other end.
This life line's body lack of sound.
Lack of sound too loud.


\*\*\*
\*\*\*
\*\*\*

I sing the criminal of those

who trespass against us on repeat.

I sing the criminal
of trespassing
outside the city's urgent care.

I sing the criminal as blues
play god on Sunday morning

as they pluck my body like a weed
from concrete into cuffs
to break the lilac
stems from profit
& the sane men shove

restraints

to make a barrier
that's able
to keep disabled

out the street
& no alarm.
Who minds

who's handcuffed
outside urgent care.
The metaphor my mouth.
Too loud, be still, I know
too well. A daisy in a cell
that no god made.

\*\*\*
\*\*\*
\*\*\*

This body. By their discourse.
An open center seedy in the wind.

\*\*\*
\*\*\*
\*\*\*

They always charge.
A sick leave on the sidewalk.

Unholy feast of city's bread
& prosecuting eyes.

The basketcase.
The fish that led the thousands.

\*\*\*
\*\*\*
\*\*\*

The meds were off.

The cops were out.
Escape hatched into ambulance.
The body patched through radar.
Scanner. Xerox Holster holding gun
as others hold their tongue. A silent
shooting star light skin. A white wall
for a body. A criminal of dopamine.
A locked jaw on the tether trace
the wire from the faucet leak.
The tap out of the ER let me loose
into their gunslung muscle.
I caught a case for losing safe rides home.
No phone no car no mind. The cops don't mind
me as I pass out here piss soaked. Solitary, single minded
state of mind, police, I felt your hands again they turned.
Their fists along my jean seams. Held my body like a victim.
Zippered teeth and zip ties two states deep
the throat chants never take it back. I can't get back
from ambulance emergent episodic bone

I held my body like a casing
in their cement corner cell.

 I held my body like a pipe dream
on their trigger on their body cam

I was a static piece electric therapy.


***
***
***


God is only criminal. I weed
through city scapes inside restraints.
I save no lives outside myself.
The blue lights fake out heaven

and clouded, white suburban comes.
Cracked up as their object
kept inside their body camera.

A basketcase the nurses chose to quick
assess, neglect, then drop. The feast

eyes in the parking lot. A legal feed
that power held. Illegal dandelion.

Illegal mind—what rose—
another word for redline
in the good book, at the jail.

Cross-wired. Press the charges like a nail.

\*\*\*
\*\*\*
\*\*\*

This is the day the lord has made I will rejoice & be glad in it
This is the day that the lord has made
That the lord has made

## Living on God's Dime

see us where the heron cops the river
for a loiter of fish mouth cuffed half-

moon yellowed evidence no questions
& no bayou but the city where we were

who watches over us & what is weaving
like stitched silver in the river the city caught

as stagnant water nearby some future crossed
its legs from fear or sense of false politeness

nearby 78 proof vessels hung
like scraps on their suburban

watch our step
& bead our sweat

what pearled
between
adidas shell
& gas pedal

to brush off town

this city wears smiles down
this city wears smiles down

cops pave themselves
authoritative as a road

to hold the body up
they hold you up

streetwise & stagger
clench their holster every time

they try to hold
some collar on the blood

white count that works
over the bones that hounds

hunting the clod out
their own raged mouth

where wages of existence is still death
what if the impulse came and went

as water wove the city
our thirst for something more
to cup than hands unlike synecdoche

some hope unlike loose change
between the heron's teeth

**A Salt**

the doe-eyed john & outskirts headlight
stubbled hem & graveled look of thorns
what splinters in the porch beams brimstones roof
our burning hands
who crossed the son off listless

sky
        & LORD the night train running someone's dress
        the cuffing season handcuffed to the light

the headlight's bulb that keeps surviving winter
white wall of an eye before the iris blooms

& when I say I am the splinter passing through
the garden & the guarded & the savior
cheap stigmata blooms your feet

again the split husk sacrament

when you think about god,
do you see three generations
        do you see the crossing silverfish
chasing the river for one minnow's worth
            do you see one bad man's silver chain
crossing the child room's bathroom counter
        another shower scene      another scheduled drug alert

another winter where I was an unfit mother unfit room
another childhood in the cotton's stained glass filter

        another filtered mouth tap water speak
        the curse/word red as god between my lips

They say I am the grl who turned around the salt

                                -hide stomach's lot of lithium
                                the pillars of our father's house
They say I am the split husk sacrament
                                the ruth ingrained & threshing


doubled over self
& huddled so                            I shake the root thick soil


I comb the sacrament of dirt        I stray hair light
upon the crossroads for the mountain

## The Patient is an Unreliable Historian
*—for Miles—*

lithium or lead, mad hatter histrionics disney movies look expensive act
according to the label in small doses stash cheek swallow good the brain
you gave away comes back tin-fold

Would you rather trope or traipse in small asylum
lithium or lead, go ask another who wars what who wore

it better in the disney movies————————— ~~hospitable you pace beneath~~
————————————————————————— ~~the liquor store unscathed~~
————————————————————————— ~~the gaitcinched off we sit~~
————————————————————————— ~~up straight in suburbs white~~

————————————————————————— ~~fence picket line of records~~
————————————————————————— ~~full of confidence & certain they~~
————————————————————————— ~~took words right out our mouths~~
—————rephrase ——————— ~~us doctors orders~~

this cartoon is ahistorical until ~~problem~~ child recites our history
waiting across the room near exit's water fountain

What brims his smile his half mouth turns

each rhymed scheme he never cared for falling loose as truth

his never
mind unlined

What departmentalized the hallway alice's wonderland

scrolls in the background San Francisco film that leaks a word we've seen
before my own bouquet on the ping pong table now I'm talking to you

telling miles how to breathe by numbers
by another's key-code door we crack a slight to let the heat thin out
to chart the tremors in another's fresh cut hand of flowers trapped

between us normal
average of our knees & bright fluor-
essence in the margins

**Traverse**

I open the curtain; I close the curtain. I go to therapy; I go to the store. I fill the intake forms in purple gel pen to make it through the inventories. Awake, all night, I remember new pieces of information. I buy a rod to assist in opening & closing the curtain. I look outside the window.

\*\*\*
\*\*\*
\*\*\*

Call me Angel. Call me Dust. I am a dime. A dime bag. Minnow. Something silver. Something silver. Sinking in the body. Of the river. Change. The men we carry in our hips. Who carry us down stream. Who carry us down stream and skim the skin. The skin. That night I was. That night I was a grl. Supposedly no angel. I treaded, tread, am treading rapids, rapid, dark; I am here again to ask you nicely: am I a wake, awake, a wake.

\*\*\*
\*\*\*
\*\*\*

I have always been called 'sensitive.' I see a stage; I stand on it. I remember my mother pulling me from the staircase: "stop crying"; "you're making this up"; or "for attention". I find a curtain to open, to close. I bow. I clap. I stand near the curtain. Some body calls this art. Some body calls this grief. Some body calls this another meaning -ful or meaning -less performance.

Some body calls my phone and it rings and rings.

\*\*\*
\*\*\*
\*\*\*

|  | snap out of it | snap fingers cracked blown piece |
|---|---|---|
| into the glass | snap out of it | laced weed & pop of PCP |

into the glass        snap out of it        snap fingers cracked bowl cherry
Babe

says any wing-man can *(flip)* on or for a dime I am a dime

bag or a minnow in the body in the river *(flip)* in quiet moments when I see your kids'
faces & *(flip)* inside the moment when you handed over their picture menacing "I'll use a
condom kiddo—" *(flip)*


\*\*\*
\*\*\*
\*\*\*


I wonder if the cashier at Arby's has trauma too. I almost ask them but instead thank
them 3 consecutive times in the drive-thru, you know, just in case. I hold my large ice
water in both hands. *Think of a cool glass of water, there are many grounding techniques—I
suggest you carry water with you when you write. when your body's had enough,* too much,
*take a sip and listen to your throat slake. taste the cool and trail it through your spine.* I have
spent five days and nights avoiding my assignment. An impact statement. Not details,
but how the incident changed, continues to change, my life.


\*\*\*
\*\*\*
\*\*\*


If I should die before I wake, *(flip)* me on my back like a good wing-man. Else err on the
side of caution tape *I'm sorry* to the mirror. Play the fault line over yes *(flip)* over & again.
I'll shave my head to skull to *(flip)* the tape the movie memory made bare. Bare back get
back *(full-stop)* & *(flip)* over & again. To *(flip)* every image that comes back in speck of
glass shoved in a hand a foot a foot-hold. *(flip)* the shattered self & fuzzy feeling. *(flip)* the
scripture that skin reels away. The skin that reels away like film like story marquee trauma
*(flip)* into the glass.

No longer on the cutting edge, shrink-wrapped I rarely come undone.

\*\*\*
\*\*\*
\*\*\*

*We'll start with the hardest, deepest rooted. if you're willing. then go from there.* To hold truth like a curtain. A little flapping lid. My eye. my I. My I: another stage. Another stage; I'm going through.

\*\*\*
\*\*\*
\*\*\*

When I walked into the white-vased room of the asylum. When my roses were at war & blooming bloodshot on the smallest dark green plastic bed. When the nurses called my halos areolas.

\*\*\*
\*\*\*
\*\*\*

*If I Should Die Before I Wake, please* (flip) *me on my back.* I'm back. No good wing-man ever made of angel dust & weed; I dust the record off. To voice over our past, play god & ghost, to ghost, to write, to ghost-write. A new version. To open the curtain. To close the curtain. The flutter in the lid. I open the curtain; I close the curtain. I go to therapy. I go to the store. Some body calls my phone.

I answer quickly when it rings.

## Every Grrl Has A Vision of Hir Ward-Robe

He said my thighs were boyish,
big, said less to crush you with.
He claimed my body was a roadmap.
Complicated to read without clear-cut
direction, without consciousness, I turned
over like a cheek & found a cig-burn
on my back's blade. He said I was a hot one,
crush of filtered, photo, semen's spring.

Splayed across the front seat, cock blocked
view of the oncoming road. When he pulled
out & over on the shoulder, I skirted strangers'
questions. O ring cheap scar smoke eye gallop
tripping over six eyes, sex legs, crushed mouth,
nip slip, evidence, so many tongues, so many

\*\*\*
\*\*\*
\*\*\*

Tongues. So many tongues to strip from shoes,
so many strings to take out bagged possessions.
Ward-Robe, white gown, white sheet, white page,
in the ward we ghost inhale & ghost exhale the thought
*if only I was King here with my idle hands pulled on the shoulder*
*waiting for headlights to flick or brain-fire to be put out.*

\*\*\*
\*\*\*
\*\*\*

We put out & we live by promises of rings

& fingers in the right spot good job G strings
are prohibited inside the ward no strings
but men here laugh say fuck me baby as I beg
the nurse to leave me nightingales say here say have a
Quiet Room they cough up a cement cell they tell
me here come cry in do not threaten, call for help.


I call for help over & over on the land line ask for the extension
of the agents of the arm of god my *King says firecrotch. Says firearm.*
*Says fired, fired, fired. I fire all the men with reclaimed wood & hobblehorse.*
*Then, some patriarchal god sweeps in & tells them* No, I got your back.

If I turn back take back buy back tonight I won't weep won't

\*\*\*
\*\*\*
\*\*\*

Weep))

        My iris
        is a waterbed
        to poke a hole in

        like a condom
        would be broken
        leak of fluid

        am I really

just a boy turned over
like a mouth
a stone inside the park
that we flip over to find
some worms in there

the wormhole is
under my body's
stone brim

like a furnace

        flip me over
        & I speak
        so many tongues

\*\*\*

\*\*\*

\*\*\*

My hobby: dress I kill & later tell it sorry,
sorry, sorry, sorry this my neckline con-
fessional why don't you scoop out every
inch of fabric of my being / my lost sheep
little boy blue ball blue in the iris my ringed
pupil yes we clouded judgement vision this
here number you can call or even number you can be
perhaps statistic call tonight if you are lonely me myself

my hot line & my vein the roofie wafer body worm
hole wound-well-open Baptists dipped their hands
in me said O my idol-grrrl my idol how many licks
years does it / will it / take & does it take the edge off
take the edge off of a blotter / white the black-out

body out / to take communion tonight my bible curled
to ash a snake's tongue splitting at the seams I locked
the four men in the fire though I only know the names
of three. Despite, for every crime I see Abednego won't burn.

**Greetings from the Future Post-Marked 1997 You**

Sometimes we'll misinterpret signs of god.
Sometimes there's no *Return Address.* Today,
I read *Disposal Church of the Redeemed*
along the shore's main drag. I heard the speech

within me: body, touch, the ground. Come to
your senses. Figurative or not, the truth's
I haven't got a thing to write us home
about. the metaphor of distant mouth

means this: the ocean's notable until
the pen drops in the outhouse. Dark, you don't
notice the foot held pools of fire ants
until the pattern formed. The morning comes.

Sun packs its heat & curious, child grasps
for magnifying glass. A suspect. Sound.

**Take Me to the Fairgrounds or the Hospital**


I figment thoroughly. I cling the plastic. I roll cigarettes
& ride across the stars. Funnel cake, a perfect storm,
sugared brain batter. Lisping frontal lobe. Horse pills
big hot air balloons. Uncurfew the ferris wheel. Lick
god's sticky fingers clean. Sky trailered taste of cotton
candy mouth in afternoon. Too full to clutch the sick
bed, bless the coasters fast release. You too must be this tall
to ride the dopamine ungutted Hand, a half dead goldfish
fooling in your open Jowl—the Body residue of weighted
bottle, a pink luck bear you pay to clutch. Don't you know who I am
by now? I'm the plush crown. I'm the carnival. I'm the light show
that's untethering. A grease fueled joy to ticket every touch.

## More Ways Than One

they played the chili peppers, sliced, prepped, cut & shuffled dinner's deck
into a stack of music, nourishment & once, we shared one name.
to one's ingredient, & background music to another. neither knew
what we meant to each other as the sound spilled out the other's mouth.

some ask us what it means to be survivors of & in the south,
to be stoned again & slack-jawed in the same comfortable bed,
slipping or agape in someone else's, reciting *those who trespassed
against us* on repeat, awaiting another hand to pluck the stalk
or else guitar string & couldn't we have washed our hands
before the burns had run along each other before we ran
our pasts along to someone else's, *scar tissue that I wish you saw,*
or did we recognize ourselves

or did we recognize us in each body then? more ways than one,
I watched the root unleash to thistle, peppered vine to scruple with
then scrap into the stove. as you made another meal. & as we knew
we only loved each other

for our ability to eat raw jalapeño whole if betted, & how much
the taste buds carried pain

& how we'd learned so young
how to hold the heat until
the tongue slid back from fire into numb.

**Full**

there are hives of honey
hives of stress red crop
circles memory's sting
no beekeeper for those
warm summer mornings

after bodies spilled their blanks into mine & the moon
that cheap machine of light I'd saved for a dark day
masked itself & slipped behind the comb of sunrise

\*\*\*
\*\*\*
\*\*\*

my grandfather was a bee keeper
he wore thick gloves & masked his hands
he looked like a boxer in the early morning dark

in the hospital my grandfather eats cheese crackers
& his orange crumb covered mouth is a baby's again
my mother combs his hair lightly with her fingers

\*\*\*
\*\*\*
\*\*\*

in the psych hospital they fed us
baloney sandwiches on stale bread
we stuffed our mouths with leftover
reasons to be alive

*parents grandparents our siblings*
*local honey in our kettled tea*

\*\*\*
\*\*\*
\*\*\*


someday I will wipe my father's chin
or ask if table manners matter to the dead
if heaven is the correct placement of a fork
on a table or a road

\*\*\*
\*\*\*
\*\*\*


this day another graveled crook
thieving my body at the intersection
like when the apple tree was split
down the middle by some lightning
& my sister cried until we broke
the homemade pie open like a prayer

\*\*\*
\*\*\*
\*\*\*


if I squint to know the moon is full
maybe I'll remember why I came here
I came here to get fed & cut the bullshit
to cut the sugar on my baby teeth

**Treatment Plans**
*after Gender Dysphoria in the DSM-5*

when the stranger/doctor/voyeur says *gimme some skin* says *hi* says *howdy* : *do you have a light*

says *do you have a marked incongruence between your experienced or expressed gender & primary
&/or secondary sex characteristics* says *do you have a strong arm* says *do you wanna wrestle
grapple* says *do you have a strong desire*
meaning *do you have a strong desire to be rid of*

says *do you have a strong desire to be rid of your primary &/or secondary sex characteristics*
says *do you have a strong desire for the primary &/or secondary sex characteristics of the other
gender*
other other other I tell my shrink
but should I tell them

I am a tree half-climbed

my body the smirk of a neighbor
my arm a bent cigarette useless to burn
my hand a wolf spider that catches the others

wrinkled up in time
I am a liturgy I tried to die
once upon a cliff by the red river

meaning I'm wary of pocket knives weary of butterflies
meaning I would like to put my body out
meaning I saw the hair on his chin and wept
meaning I'm considering initializing change

as a child doubles over the stubble
of grass waiting under winter—
the ice melts with the last emergency
contact in my phone

when the stranger/doctor/voyeur says *do you have a strong desire to be*

*of the other gender do you have a strong desire to be treated*
*as the other gender do you have a strong conviction you have typical feelings*
do you have typical feelings do you have typical reactions
*do you have the typical feelings & reactions of the other gender*
I say weekly

somebody rubs
my body out
& I disperse

the vial half full of a voice
I cannot drop into the undergrowth

& maybe I'm going
under the knife
to sing with other angels
we have heard on high
& maybe I'm going under
the knife to sing saying I have

the habit of saying things sometimes

like I wish that you could see
the lake today but you keep asking
do you see a clear blue eye

**Third Space (Cowboys)**

My boy says we're gravitational. We all have pulls. Matter. Mass. Energy.
It's scientific. We have systems. We have horizontal knowledge.

We have bodies that do queer shit. Unlike language, we revolve.


My boy they are a god's eye with no strings attached together.
We're out of step inside this figment that we live imaginary
boxer cardboard cut-up tranarchy. Denotation/Connotation.
The space some "what" between.

Some say Roadkill. We say Queer Steer. We say Doe-thick velvet.
Antlers of no matter. Buck.          *Was it sudden when you hit that? Was it sudden when*
*the fog lifted?*

((Rhinestone the Butch Cassidy in me does not mean a lasso is not rope.
A lasso is a noose unsprung, something a cowboy left behind.))


But I ain't got a cock like his so he calls me Golden Laurel.

He calls me animal in bed (river, mattress, bright red pick-up).

You say roadkill. We say Queer Steer. We say Doe-thick velvet.

Antlers


of no matter. We say Buck.

Say body never asked but gladly given—God—

which is to say—Once at the creek past midnight someone mis-
interpreted my revolution as his revolver. Threatened by my body,
he boxed me in & tried to attack "back".

                    He said I'd never be more than a—

Sudden screech of breaks.
My quick lit glimpse of wisdom
& my spinny whiplashed neck.


We carry on our roadkill. We carry on. Trail blaze.
This doe-thick pupil Queer Steer. Wheel
turn. Rear view. Mirror. Horn


& stubbled happy trail. Say buck. Say antlers of no matter.
Rack.  Say Antlers. Rack. Say antlers. Buck. Say Buck—


which is to say—Last night a cowboy won the rodeo
& he let his horse loose in that same old creek.
The horse's name was Sugar & he had just let her run free.
When he found us on the creek bank, he was hollering
for her return. Drunk, and on a mission, he told us


to please send love
if we happened to cross her.


*Sugar in my mouth & the word tastes sweet*
*like every speech we patterned in the bed*
*knowing water'd leave it fluid*


*lickety split tongue chant of neck & bow & ribbon candy*
*taste bud blossom mine & thine & Sugar another word for rope*
*untethered another name*
*for let's get on & ride*


*my Sugar a mouth that swept the river*
*Sugar a mythic beast in bumfuck*
*Sugar another beast like me*


*Sugar another hoofbeat blessed*

& Sugar, what we ride on

**Visual Cliff**

Specialists claim we all believe in cliffs once we reach crawling age.
This week I've been back on my knees & running like an engine
trying not to drive their point into the ground. It is winter & a fog
machine keeps hanging out my mouth. The stakes myself beside myself
the ragged party streamer of a river. Each breath some fog machine
on this abandoned bridge. A song I don't remember looping like thread
above, below, through trees, through you & me: a misplaced lyric
hummed along as memory is shifting with the distance.

It seems that the song kicks the wind out of you
or that you kick the wind out of the song.

It seems that I keep saying *thank god for the trees.*
& Thank god for the trees. You know what my God says?

*Shit crops up sometimes. Get back to work.*

**It Was Always Us!**
*after Kalyn Fay Barnoski*

it was always us!

in the kitchen, in the check out, in the check in, in the checked box, in the checkered shoes & cheeks turned toward a kiss along the check out line, in the wave hello and wave of water, in the creek gap & the gapped tooth, in the mouth tongue & the toothpaste, in the sink drain, in the rain & sun.

it was always us!

in the lighthouse, in the forest, in the cabin, in the duplex, in the duplicated hands we hold together, in the silence, in the prayer and in the drumline in the holler in the valley made, the holding cell, the waiting room, the wait a minute, & the fuck it—go—in the action, in the mirror, in the lightswitch, in the planter & the window.

it was always us!

in the cabinets, in the woodgrain, in the winter, in the flicker, in the peonies & the corner's change, in the street sign, in the stop light, in the picket, in the stray hair & the pillow, in the birds nest, in the feather, in the garden, in the ladybug, the lavender, the dirt bed & the mattress springs.

it was always us!

in the yarn hooks, in the staked plot, in the gravel, in the diner, in the flashlight, in the garden shed & skin shed, in the rusted & the water can, in the drainpipe, in the corner, in the hoodie & the temple, in the leghair & the denim, in the leather vest & spike of temperature.

it was always us!

in the bike ride, in the weather, in the late night, in the drivethru, in the driveby, in the dine, in the backseat & the parking lot, the space some numbered & some ticketed, the infinite & clouded sky, the blue lights & the backfire of moon, the big dipper & the dip of hip, the smoke, the trees, the razor burn, the split lip & the wisdom tooth.

it was always us!

the knot of muscle & the joined red string, the clay & river & the blushed cheek & the wheel turned toward a gravel road.

it was always us!

in the check out, in the check in, in the passing cars & passed notes, in the ozarks, in the hand-me-downs & handwrittens, in the language & the speechless, in the cities, in the growing fields, the shower & the curtain, in the houses and the complexes, in the crickets & the wind chimes, in the breezes and the weather vane.

it was always us!

another's foot hold to another's step, in a lifeline without fathom, in the center of your hand, & in the heart line without matter & a generationless refrain.

past the body moves the vessel. we move in & out of classrooms psych wards prisons skin cells court rooms lunch lines bathrooms back alleys bath houses kitchens dance halls bars friends houses gas stations intersections forked roads skylines creekbeds mountains biketrails taxis stop lights food trucks sidewalks grass lawns oceans water constellations skylines

it was always us! it was always us! it was always us.

**Love Radical**

as water as spit
toothpaste into the drain

as Epsom salt as lavender
as bristle & the brush

of love to love tonight
take Epsom salt to psalm the feet

let joy abolish fear & kiss
someone yourself your hands

breathe in breathe out again
sing a song only the mad canaries can

undone unraveled trip of lavender & daylight
bask in every revolution fold of skin

& fat & hip & cellulite & energized
say fuck the power bill say fuck the power

say fuck the rent say fuck the landlord
say fuck the landlord's father too

turn off the news
turn on the radio

& shake it thru the living room

make home here
where yr body is

say pennies lie
peonies grow

take grain of salt into the shower

**Aubade for Possums, Waking, Sweet as Them—**

I woke up to the porch's scuffle. Noise
& smell of apple core, our one-month old,
the trash beneath our twin. I woke up grateful
for visitors of late & godly hours—

humid & half-lit AM, sweet as home
we cherish, see, & hold. other/s refuse
to see the miracle of rug that reeked
on porch near scrap tin feeder. squint of dawn

where fists of loose birdseed have spilled then sprouted
in rain drenched cloth—the stitches, saplings—strange
a possum's gentle vows—I'll sweep for ticks,
will heap my loves inside myself, heart's hiss

a roadside kind of animal, instinctual & welcomed here.
Collective nuzzled heap, figure of speech.

**Where/Did You Sleep Last Night**

is joy the cattail edge
far past the holler

the birdsong brush
along the mouth
between

us
valleys hillside rolling
eyes

what throat
could overlook
the trees

seedlings
could sprout
along the hollers gap

tongue whistled thru
the future
grasses not unraveled there

the dirt mound rocking
what skulls left
remains

herein
to tap
the stifled

little root
& touch
the base

of limbline
soul
what pines

this moss
across the balded field

I soar
as eagle
angel

just above us
rings

topsoil
to bottomed worm
to catch

what my mouth cups
along the byway

trail sounds lure
what none thought edible:

see-through,
the forest comes.

moist eyes running back
all mossing toward the sun.

**Only God or Google Knows Why the King's River's Running Backwards**

*(a cupped hand in the psych ward shower isn't prayer.*
*I mothed a song into the fickle light)*

they say it was an earthquake or a bad trip in the mirror
to know the crown of crows along the bank as same as forehead

that pinecone opens/closes. adaptive/economic heart.

even with temperature the hinge will swell or freeze
there like a memory. tremors in my fistheap as I take

the stand. fruit city sold for cheap. I hear that jesus walked

on water then they strung him out in thorns. I bet he'd walk
King's River like a backwards escalator. takes more time

to perform miracles this winter. blessed streetwise dandelion
in the ice storm. snowmobile threads salt.

plot-thick when radar comes. who gives a fuck
about frost or the poem.

blue jays fly and whistle at the same time near the sidewalk.
& you a gate of teeth that never speaks.

jesus didn't believe in upward mobility
until he rose up one spring like a lily.

this a crossguard for the children. school of fish
& state's disciplespeak. something flipped

the switch on him. another unpaid lightbill. a thousand
dollar visit. threat of the electric. carceral men of myrrh & thorazine.

we built our infrastructure byway
of parable & document. advisory of every road's condition

on the backpocketed cell. a chain of collars blue to white
as heaven. chainlink of events. what led some scientist to name

these red birds cardinals. the music walked the water then

reverbed the crown again. natural disaster in the river
not the rocksong. when the water flipped out, it never was

the same. commodity of christlike. I cross/keep
the stream that flips between my tongue and teeth.

## Acknowledgements

I'm grateful to Open Mouth Literary Center's residency program & the Writer's Colony at Dairy Hollow for space to organize and revise my manuscript.

## Previous Publications

"Babylon" appears in Typo Magazine.
"Chromosomes to Name the Wild" appears in The Rupture.
 "Full" appears in New South Journal.
"Every Grrl Has a Vision of Hir Ward-Robe" appears in Crab Fat Magazine.
"Holy Rollers" appears in Mississippi Review.
"In Danger (To Myself & Others" appears in Sprung Formal.
"Living on God's Dime" appears in Muzzle Magazine.
"Mad in America" appears in Stone of Madness.
"Take Me To the Fairgrounds or the Hospital" & "More Ways Than One" appear in Diode Poetry Journal.
"Third Space (Cowboys)" appears in Gigantic Sequins.
"Thorazine at 10:00 am" appears in Poetry Magazine.
"Where/Did You Sleep Last Night" appears in Columbia Review.
Previous versions of several of these poems appeared as "Shrinking the Violet" in Crab Fat Magazine.
"Traverse", "Every Grrl Has A Vision of Hir Ward-Robe" & "Full" were previously published in the chapbook *Boyish* (Omnidawn Publishing, May 2021).

## Gratitude

I'm grateful to Rusty & everyone at Omnidawn for shifting this book from thought into the tangible, for unwavering support, kindness, & solidarity.

I'm grateful to Lynette Thrower and the artist response cohort with *Nick Cave: Until* at the Momentary for inspiring several of the poems in this collection.

I'm grateful to Kalyn Fay Barnoski's group exhibit *It Was Always Us!* for inspiring and including the responsive poem "It Was Always Us!" that was shown as a large-scale print in 2021. "It Was Always Us" was first performed on the steps of the Arkansas Capitol at Rally for Trans Rights, where many Arkansas community members and organizations gathered to combat anti-trans legislation in March 2021. I am grateful to the nurses for writing "the patient is an unreliable historian" in my intake notes at Brentwood Hospital in 2008, if only for relearning what it means to hold the power of narrative as a mad queer person navigating institutions & societal pressures to dampen my voice. I am grateful to Max, above all, for holding that space close with me and every love between.

I am blessed beyond measure by the loving memory of Matt Henriksen who played an integral role in shaping how I continue to show up in the world. As he said:

> "…we are at once dancing and grieving
> in the fire that drapes us as a flag
> to wear as long as we can stand
> as decoys so that others might
> be allowed to speak their way out
> of a fire that is not their flag"

**Brody Parrish Craig** (they/them) is the author of *Boyish*, which won the 2019 Omnidawn Poetry Chapbook Contest. Their writing has appeared in *Muzzle Magazine, Poetry, Mississippi Review, New South, Missouri Review* and *TYPO,* among others. They are the editor of *TWANG,* a regional anthology of TGNC+ creators from the south/midwest. A 2022 recipient of Artist 360's Community Activator Award, they currently co-lead TLGBQ+ community arts programming with their husband Maximiliano Calabotta in the Ozarks.

The Patient is an Unreliable Historian
by Brody Parrish Craig

Cover design by Maximiliano Calabotta & Joshua R. Johnson
Cover typeface: Garamond
Interior design by Laura Joakimson
Interior typeface: Warnock Pro and Adobe Garamond


Printed in the United States
by Books International,
Dulles, Virginia on Acid Free Archival Quality Recycled Paper


Publication of this book was made possible in part by gifts from Katherine &
John Gravendyk in honor of Hillary Gravendyk,
Francesca Bell, Mary Mackey, and The New Place Fund


Omnidawn Publishing Oakland, California
Staff and Volunteers, Fall 2024
Rusty Morrison & Laura Joakimson, co-publishers
Rob Hendricks, poetry & fiction editor,
& post-pub marketing
Jeffrey Kingman, copy editor
Sharon Zetter, poetry editor & book designer
Anthony Cody, poetry editor
Liza Flum, poetry editor
Kimberly Reyes, poetry editor
Elizabeth Aeschliman, fiction & poetry editor
Rayna Carey, marketing assistant
Kailey Garcia, marketing assistant
Jennifer Metsker, marketing assistant
Katie Tomzynski, marketing assistant
Sophia Carr, production editor